TINTINHULL HOUSE GARDEN

Somerset

The National Trust

Tintinhull

A formal garden informally planted

'My garden is, I think and hope, a happy one.' Who could disagree with Phyllis Reiss, who created here between 1933 and 1961 one of the most harmonious and carefully thought-out small gardens in Britain?

Mrs Reiss's starting-point was the house, which was built in the early 18th century from the local Ham Hill stone – the same stone that forms the flagstone paths through the garden. From the windows of Tintinhull House, she could look out over not one, but six gardens, arranged in a formal grid pattern. Despite Tintinhull's flat site and modest scale (less than two acres), these roughly rectangular courtyards have very different characters – from the small paved enclosure of the Fountain Garden to the more open lawn of the Pool Garden. Like Hidcote, they are separated by high hedges and mellow brick walls, but linked by a complex web of vistas, which end in garden sculpture or seats, where you are welcome to rest.

Mrs Reiss took just as much care in planting as in planning, choosing varieties which would provide exciting combinations of colour and scent throughout the season. As the garden designer Lanning Roper wrote, 'Her special gift was for selecting and placing plants to create an effect. If a plant is distinguished in form and texture it is used boldly and often repeated, this making a unity of design.' Since 1954 the National Trust has kept that spirit alive. Nowhere is this better seen than in the Pool Garden. Here in the summer, one of the mixed herbaceous borders is filled with bold

colours – verbascums, yellow achillea, *Senecio* 'Sunshine', red 'Frensham' roses and copper-foliaged plants, such as *Cotinus coggygria*. In the other, the gentler pinks of phlox and *Penstemon* 'Hidcote Pink' and the violets of *Campanula lactiflora* predominate. Like all the planting at Tintinhull, the contrast is perfectly judged.

Lilium 'Golden Splendor'. Mrs Reiss had a particular love of lilies

(*Left*) Mrs Reiss conceived her garden as a series of separate 'rooms' linked by vistas – here from the Kitchen Garden across the Pool Garden

(*Above right*) Lady's mantle, campanula and the crimson *Rosa gallica* on the steps between the Pool Garden and the Kitchen Garden

The Nappers of Tintinhull

The Dissolution of the Monasteries in the 1530s meant rich pickings for those with influence at Court. One such was Henry VIII's Secretary of State, Sir William Petre, who acquired the manors of Montacute and nearby Tintinhull. In 1546 he assigned the tenancy of the Tintinhull parsonage (now called The Court) to an old Oxford friend, Edward Napper, so beginning that family's 250-year association with the village. As Tintinhull's glove-making industry prospered, so did the Nappers, who built new houses in the village for their children.

Tintinhull House

The earliest surviving part of the house is the east front, through which you enter today. It was built by 1630, when that date and the initial 'N' for Napper were carved into the gable end. Not surprisingly, the Nappers chose Ham Hill stone, from which Montacute and the rest of Tintinhull are also built. For it attracts speckled lichen and glows golden in the sunlight.

In 1722 Andrew Napper extended the house to the west by adding a new five-bay entrance front. He topped it with a classically correct pediment and hipped roof of stone slates, but decided to have stone window mullions rather than the more fashionable and practical wooden sash-windows. Because of its perfectly judged proportions, the west front looks bigger than it actually is, and has inspired many imitations, including a house built in Atlanta, Georgia, in 1918, which was christened Somerset House in its honour. To provide a suitably impressive approach to his new front, Napper added the fore-court walls and eagles at the same time.

Later History

By 1746 the Napper family was shrinking in numbers and wealth, and the house was being let out to the Pitt family. Ruined by a life of extravagance, John Napper died deep in debt in 1791, forcing his widow to sell Tintinhull House. It passed through several hands until 1835, when it was bought by Jeremiah Penny, a local farmer whose family lived here for the rest of the 19th century.

Arthur Cobbett, who bought Tintinhull in 1898, added the single-storey extension to the east front, but seems to have used the house little, finally emigrating to South Africa and selling to his tenant, Dr S.J.M. Price. The writer Llewelyn Powys remembered Price as 'small and frail in appearance, but possessed of a Spartan spirit' with a 'wan sensitive smile'. Price was a distinguished botanist, who let valerian, rue and other native herbs grow freely around the garden. He also put down the patterned flagstones in Eagle Court and the Middle Garden, and may have sought advice from the garden designer Harold Peto, who lived nearby at Iford Manor and whose sister was a friend.

(*Left*) The elegant west front was added to the house in 1722

The Court was the Nappers' main house in Tintinhull

Creating the Garden

'What fun one has trying things – my hopes always soar to great heights when planning and planting, only very often to be dashed later on – but one complete success is worth many failures, and I am grateful for having a lovely old garden to work in – also for our soft western climate.'

Phyllis Reiss, 1939

Phyllis Reiss and her husband, Capt. F.E. Reiss, bought Tintinhull in 1933. She had served her gardening apprenticeship at Dowdeswell Manor near Cheltenham, and, as she cheerfully admitted to the gardening writer Fred Whitsey, 'made her mistakes there'. Now she would have nothing in her second garden that did not fit into the planting schemes she had devised. Dowdeswell was also close to Lawrence Johnston's famous garden at Hidcote, and his subtle mixture of garden 'rooms', complex interlinked vistas and rich planting was to be an important influence on Tintinhull.

The west front of the house already determined the main axis of the garden, which stretches away from the central doorway. Mrs Reiss extended the garden to the north by creating Cedar Court from what had been a rough paddock. In 1947 she converted the adjoining tennis court into the Pool Garden, which was also carefully linked to the Middle and Kitchen Gardens with new vistas.

Above all, Mrs Reiss wanted her garden to be a peaceful place, in which people could sit and relax. So she placed garden seats where they could appreciate in comfort the complex effects she had created. She enjoyed showing visitors round, always ending up in the Pool Garden summer-house, where she would sit on summer evenings looking out over her garden and analysing what worked and what didn't with great care. In a BBC talk in 1939 she explained: 'As the layout is flat and overlooked from most of the rooms in the house, my main object in planning and planting is to make it as interesting as possible all the year round.' She was not interested in rarities for their own sake, but in combining plants in unexpected ways, such as putting Darwin tulips among blue Dutch irises, backed by delphiniums and clumps of her favourite *Lilium regale* in Eagle Court. She called herself a 'groupist', as opposed to a 'plantist' ('I generally try and plant two things together'), and she was not afraid of repeating plants, if they were successful: 'I can't bear any place to be void of flower and colour over a long period.'

Mrs Reiss generously gave the house and garden to the National Trust in 1954, continuing to live here until her death in 1961. Almost her last act in the garden was to plant another cedar in Cedar Court to carry on the tradition when the mature tree eventually died – as, sadly, it did in 1994.

The National Trust has now looked after Mrs Reiss's garden for more than two-thirds of its existence, and has inevitably made changes, as no garden can stand still. Between 1980 and 1993 Tintinhull was lucky enough to have the leading garden designer and writer Penelope Hobhouse as its tenant. She introduced many new ideas, making a special effort to enrich the planting of the terracotta pots which are such a useful element in a comparatively small garden like Tintinhull. The present Gardener-in-Charge, Floyd Summerhayes, continues to experiment, while remaining true to Mrs Reiss's tradition of thoughtful planting.

The tranquil Pool Garden was perhaps Mrs Reiss's most inspired creation

Tour of the Garden

The Courtyard

Mrs Reiss believed that the approach to a garden should be relatively austere, giving little or no hint of what is to come. A wooden door in the courtyard wall, generally left open, allows a welcoming glimpse of Cedar Court. For a few days in early summer, the south-facing wall of the old stone barn turns blue with the flowers of a massive old wisteria. For most of the year interest comes from the shape of the plants and the play of light upon stone.

The West Terrace

Your first sight of the garden is the main axis path centred on the west façade, framed in the Drawing Room doorway. As you step from the relative gloom of the Drawing Room on to the steps leading down to the West Terrace, you can begin to appreciate the full impact of the garden.

The planting on the West Terrace is largely confined to containers – four large stone pots, which contain Mrs Reiss's original planting scheme of *Lilium regale*. Given plenty of feeding with liquid tomato feed and a kind season, these can produce up to twenty of their sweetly scented white flower spikes per pot.

Eagle Court

The first garden – really a courtyard – is enclosed by brick walls added about 1720, at the same time as the west façade. The central, diamond-patterned stone path lined with large box domes is all that remains of Dr Price's garden. Mrs Reiss skilfully incorporated this important element of his garden into her design.

The south-facing borders on the right contain a wonderful edging of alternating

Deep violet *Clematis* 'Etoile Violette' covers the wall dividing Eagle Court from the Middle Garden

clumps of the sapphire blue *Agapanthus umbellatus* and the later-flowering pink *Nerine bowdenii*. At various points this is broken by single plants of *Lavandula* × *intermedia* 'Grappenhall', providing a visual link with the two small borders of *Lavandula angustifolia* 'Hidcote'. On the warm south-facing walls ceanothus, magnolia, coronilla and clematis flourish. On the lower wall, the original gate pillar supports a tapestry of pale blue *Clematis* 'Prince Charles' intertwined with deep violet *Clematis* 'Etoile Violette' and *Lonicera periclymenum*.

In spring these borders are awash with the yellow tulip 'West Point' and wallflower 'Primrose Monarch', complementing the acid yellow heads of *Euphorbia characias* ssp. *wulfenii*. Mrs Reiss was fond of hybrid tea and the much newer floribunda roses – hence the two groups of rose 'Peace', and a pair of tall, lemon yellow rose 'High Noon' standing sentinel in front of the house.

Other plants to look out for in the summer are the tall, pale primrose spires of *Alcea rugosa* and *Salvia turkestanica* with its papery pinkish-blue bracts. The lime green bells of *Nicotiana langsdorffii* are a perfect companion to the primrose daisies of *Anthemis tinctoria* 'Wargrave'.

On the left, the cooler, more shaded borders contain some fine specimens of scented philadelphus, hydrangeas and *Itea ilicifolia*, underplanted with *Geranium nodosum* and *Helleborus orientalis*. The border edging is *Bergenia cordifolia* and *Aster divaricatus*, a particular favourite of the Edwardian garden designer Gertrude Jekyll. These borders also contain two classic 1930s garden trees – *Prunus* 'Ukon' and *Malus hupehensis*.

The Drawing Room door frames a view of the box domes in Eagle Court and the Middle Garden. A garden seat in the Fountain Garden closes the vista

In May the old barn in the courtyard is almost hidden by a wisteria

Pink *Geranium palmatum* flowers beneath the reproduction Kent urn in the Middle Garden

In spring cherry blossom fills the entrance to the Middle Garden from the Pool Garden

The Middle Garden

Much less carefully arranged than Eagle Court, the Middle Garden has a quieter and more natural feel, with no defined colour scheme. It is overlooked by the pair of stone eagles perched on top of the original gate pillars.

In the 1930s, when Mrs Reiss came to Tintinhull, most of this garden was a paddock, but within these boundaries were five mature trees, including the pair of *Quercus ilex*. These trees gave the emerging garden height and dappled shade created by moving leaves. The north-facing border is being replanted with Mrs Reiss's original late spring scheme of largely Kurme azaleas underplanted with *Lilium martagon* var. *album*. Towards the far end of this border a copy of an 18th-century William Kent urn on a pedestal forms one end of perhaps the most famous vista at Tintinhull, through to the summer-house in the Pool Garden. The south-facing shrub border forms a less defined boundary and screens the Pool Garden from immediate view.

The Fountain Garden

At the far end of the Middle Garden, the diamond-patterned path ends in a short flight of steps leading down into the Fountain Garden. This area, divided by tall yew hedges, forms a series of gardens within a garden. The first has a gold theme, originally being planted with *Azalea lutea*; due to the dry conditions created by the roots of the *Quercus*, most have been replaced by *Philadelphus coronarius* 'Aureus'. During the spring, these beds overflow with *Scilla siberica*.

Enclosed by yew hedges, the interior planting scheme of white remains virtually hidden until the last moment. The central feature is a circular lily pool with a simple fountain, which was restored during the winter of 1996–7 thanks to a substantial donation from the late Miss Hardwick. During the restoration, the original fountain head was uncovered. It produces a single jet of water which allows waterlilies to flower. The planting scheme is quite formal, repeating groups of plants, such as *Iris* 'White City' and *Rosa* 'Iceberg'. Because the beds are so small, the planting tends to be in blocks rather than in more naturally merging groups.

Beyond the central fountain area lies a small foliage garden. The white metal seat is framed by a clipped bay arch, giving a wonderful view back to the house. It was donated by the Nurses League of Birmingham General Hospital in memory of Penelope Hobhouse's husband, the late Professor John Malins. The choice of foliage plants is largely inspired by the pair of *Cornus controversa* 'Variegata' with their wonderful layered branches. Until shortly after the Second World War, Captain Reiss's garden shed stood here.

'Iceberg' roses and other white-flowering plants predominate in the Fountain Garden

The Kitchen Garden

During Mrs Reiss's lifetime, visitors were not allowed into the Kitchen Garden. Like many people at that time, she believed vegetables were for eating, not looking at. Hence all the views into the Kitchen Garden are lined with flower borders. The path from the centre of the Fountain Garden through the Kitchen Garden is lined with *Nepeta* 'Six Hills Giant'. The cross path contains *Rosa* 'Nathalie Nypels', backed by espalier pears and *Lonicera halliana* scrambling over upright supports.

Captain Reiss had a passion for pears and is thought to have grown them here as espaliers. In early summer he would give 100 muslin bags to Mrs Mapletoft (the wife of the then Head Gardener) to check for holes and repair. He then placed them over the most promising young pears as some protection against pests, both animal and human.

Following Mrs Reiss's death, the National Trust decided to keep the Kitchen Garden productive. This adds greatly to the feeling of a complete garden, so typical of a small country house. As produce is not needed for the house these days, we grow a much wider range of vegetables, fruit, herbs and cut flowers, to give a flavour of what this area would have been like. Nowadays, much of it is sold to visitors.

In a relatively small space, crop rotations are not strictly followed. Each spring, the planting starts in a different bed, and vegetables, herbs and most of the annual cut flowers are grown in rows side by side. This random approach to planting gives a very cottage garden feel, and looking across the beds from different angles can give some wonderful foliage contrasts. In recent years a small amount of each variety has been allowed to run to seed, to form next year's crop. Most modern varieties tend to mature at the same time, making a succession much more difficult, but if left to seed in this way, they will tend to revert to the old stock and give a longer cropping period.

From the spring of 1999, a small area has been used to produce vegetable seed under the Henry Doubleday Heritage Seed Library Gardens Scheme. This seed library contains hundreds of varieties, most of which have fallen foul of EU legislation and cannot be sold to gardeners within Europe. The crops of seed from these plants are returned to the Henry Doubleday Institute, which can then give small amounts to their members.

(*Above*) Cabbages and flowering nepeta

(*Below*) The pink rose 'Nathalie Nypels' lines the path through the Kitchen Garden

Mauve catmint abounds in the Kitchen Garden

The Pool Garden

The Pool Garden is probably the best remembered of Mrs Reiss's planting schemes and forms the centrepiece of the garden. Until 1947 this area was a tennis court. Mrs Reiss raised £500 by the sale of an old cider orchard and used the money to lay out this garden, including the canal and summer-house. She dedicated it to the memory of her nephew Michael Lucas, a Fleet Air Arm fighter pilot killed on one of the Malta convoys in 1945.

To the eye, this garden appears symmetrical; in fact, there is a definite slant to the south. This is disguised by the overall design and is enhanced by mowing the grass panels on the diagonal. As with the rest of the garden, these panels are not exactly rectangular.

The summer-house provides welcome shade and a place to sit and enjoy the swallows swooping over the water. The locally made willow seats are dedicated to the memory of George Mapletoft, Gardener at Tintinhull for 40 years. In recent years the inside of the summer-house has been enhanced with terracotta pots and shade-loving hardy perennials and ferns, such as *Rodgersia tabularis*, *Zantedeschia* and hostas. From here, you can compare the distinctive colour schemes of the contrasting east and west borders. Until early summer, colour and texture in these borders is achieved by the use of foliage plants common to both, and in the spring they are vibrant with tulips, giving a hint of the colour schemes to come.

The west border scheme is based around strong colours, with plenty of reds and yellows. Four clumps of crimson red *Rosa* 'Frensham' provide continuity. By high summer, the border sizzles with *Achillea* 'Gold Plate', salvias, *Lilium henryi*, *Clematis recta* and deep blue delphiniums. Towards the end of the season, groups of dahlias and asters provide a grand finale.

The opposite, east border planting is based around much cooler blues, mauves and pinks. New plantings of pale blush pink *Rosa* 'Many Happy Returns' will fulfil the same role as the *Rosa* 'Frensham' opposite. The soft light of early morning and late evening brings out the colours of the roses, delphiniums, campanulas and *Galega*. By late summer, groups of dahlias and asters take over in both borders. From the seat in the middle of the east border, you get a fine view of the Kitchen Garden roses framed by an archway cut in the yew hedge opposite.

Containers play a very important role at Tintinhull, and particularly in this garden. Their style of planting still owes much to the influence of Penelope Hobhouse. The pots are planted twice annually. For the spring display, we use various combinations of tulips, wallflowers and pansies. In May these are replaced with a mixture of annuals and tender perennials.

The brilliant red climbing rose 'Allen Chandler' on the summer-house

The yellow flag iris, *Iris pseudocorus*, and waterlilies fill the pool

The armillary sphere in the west border is surrounded by the contrasting textures of self-seeded *Eryngium giganteum* and large-leaved *Crambe cordifolia*

Cedar Court

This was the first area Captain and Mrs Reiss set about developing, from what had been a rough paddock, with a muddy path running along the north wall of the house. Early in 1993 the large Cedar of Lebanon, which stood against the south-facing garden wall, was found to be seriously infected with Honey Fungus, and in February 1994 it had to be felled. A replacement was planted in the lawn in 1995. We took the opportunity to realign the garden paths and so ease wear and tear on the lawns. With the old tree gone and the path straightened, a new border was created after thoroughly sterilising the soil. Unlike the majority of Tintinhull's borders, there is no set planting scheme. Instead, we have introduced here plants that had disappeared from the garden over the years, and will allow the design to evolve gradually, as Mrs Reiss's original borders did.

Fronting the yew hedge which divides Cedar Court from the Pool Garden, is the purple border. This was the first border Mrs Reiss created at Tintinhull, and purple foliage seems to have been very important to her. The backbone of this scheme is a number of different purple-leaved berberis. This general colouring is carried through into the rose cultivars, such as 'Rosemary Rose', and many of the herbaceous plants have pink or blue flowers which complement these.

In the spring of 1995, thanks to the generosity of the author Susan Hill, we were able to replant the narrow iris border with the original cultivars. Unfortunately, irises are prone to numerous diseases and are a constant struggle to maintain, but the stunning yellow, bronze and mahogany blooms make a spectacular, if fleeting, display.

The taller walls of Cedar Court provide some shelter for a small collection of magnolias. The warm south-facing wall protects a young *Magnolia grandiflora*, which in time will clothe a large section of the wall. Close to this, set in the lawn, is a specimen *Magnolia* × *soulangeana*, underplanted with the autumn-flowering *Cyclamen hederifolium*. When these are not in flower, there is a wonderful range of leaf patterns and shapes to provide interest. Next to the broad north terrace are two very large specimens of *Magnolia liliiflora* 'Nigra'. Although their peak flowering is in the spring, odd flowers can be found throughout the year.

The view from Cedar Court towards the Fountain Garden